SACRAMENTO PUBLIC LIBRARY

D0753271

3 3029 00840

WITHDRAWN FROM COLLECTION
OF SACRAMENTO PUBLIC LIBRARY

CENTRAL

APR 82

SACRAMENTO PUBLIC LIBRARY
SACRAMENTO, CALIFORNIA

Abdul-Hamid's Palestine

frontispiece
Letter of an Armenian photographer in Jerusalem accompanying an album of photographs presented to Abdul-Hamid II. The letter is composed of formulas of respect and adulation, ending in "Your slave, Karabet Krikorian, a photographer in Jerusalem." At the top is the seal of the Imperial Library, with the *tughra* in its upper part

endpapers dyestamp
Tughra of Sultan Abdul-Hamid II. The *tughra* was the sultan's own stylized signature, and every sultan had an individual one. A number of specially appointed artist-scribes had the exclusive duty of drawing it, and it always came at the top of official documents, so that nothing would be written above it. The *tughra* shown here is a particularly fine example

و ذي حشمت وقدرت ولي النعمت يكتا جدِّ اعدل واكرم اشهر عالم افندمز حضرتلرينك يوم ليلة برابری شوكت و سلطنت بيوريورلر ايها

ده و عنايات به جنابِ خلافت نصيب نظير مظهر و اوغور ميامنه موفور شهريارلريلر نده فداى جانه حاضر اولان هر عبد صادقه وسيع واقتدا ايا خراكی

جمهوريت و وظيفهٔ نظيفهٔ سيله مكلف اولوب دنياره مدارسه ده وواسطهٔ يگانهٔ مضرهٔ انجوم التفات به جهان داور به ولى النعم عظيمه

بو عبد درمحرر يه كرى كمالِ عجز وافتقار ايله سنه متعدده دنبرى اشتغال ايديكى صنعتمكترا سنك لائق اولان محصولیِ نشول

جسارت ايديور امر و فرمان به دهلهٔ رشاد علياسناه و شنشاه رحمت اكناه ولى النعمت عالمِ السلطان زاد الله فيومه حضرتلريكده ر

قنسطنطينه
ليتوغرافيه كردستكه لي ككي
قناری

Abdul-Hamid's Palestine

Rare century-old photographs from the
private collection of the Ottoman sultan
now published for the first time

Selected and introduced by

Jacob M. Landau

جناب رتبهٔال پادشاه معليخصا

سايجها وايٰ مملكدار عظميلر ندهم رد

درجه سنده خاكياى مرحم احتواى هيهد

عبار بدكو رله وتبصيح برامل ومطلو

لخاطه جناب شهريار عظمى بويلوراشت

ANDRE DEUTSCH

First published 1979 by
André Deutsch Limited
105 Great Russell Street London WCI

ISBN 0 233 97135 .1

Library of Congress Catalog
Card Number: 78-73701

All rights reserved. No part of this publication may be reproduced, stored in a
retrieval system, or transmitted, in any form or by any means, electronic,
mechanical, photocopying, recording or otherwise, without the prior permission
of the copyright owner.

Designed by Alex Berlyne

Copyright © 1979 Carta, Jerusalem

Set by Isratypset, Jerusalem
Printed by Peli Printing Works, Ltd.
Printed in Israel

Contents

Acknowledgements

I would like to thank the librarians of the University Library in Istanbul for kindly allowing me to browse through the collections of photographs of Abdul-Hamid II and to select those of interest to me; Mr. M. M. Işin, of Istanbul, who prepared half-tone negatives from the photographs selected; Mr. Emanuel Hausman and the staff of Carta, Jerusalem, for their unflagging courtesy in all stages of publication; Mr. Alex Berlyne, for his design and expert advice; and Ms. Ina Friedman, for her capable editing of the text. I am also grateful for comments and assistance, at various stages of my work, to my son Iddo, Professor Shmuel Tamari, and Dr. Zev Vilnay. All of the above have helped to improve this book and it has been a pleasure, indeed, to work with them. Any errors of fact or interpretation that remain are my own.

Jerusalem   Jacob M. Landau
September 1976

Introduction

In order better to grasp the message of the following photographs, one should first know something about the Ottoman sultan of the time, his empire, and most particularly Palestine.

Abdul-Hamid II was undoubtedly one of the most controversial sultans to rule the Ottoman Empire. His thirty-three years on the throne (1876–1909) witnessed a critical period for the empire. These were the days when Czars Alexander III and Nicholas II were the autocratic rulers of Russia; Queen Victoria was reigning over a far-flung British Empire; the Third Republic in France was still striving to recoup from the defeat of 1870–71; and Bismarck was governing the affairs of a recently united Germany. All of these and others were following events in the Ottoman Empire closely. Abdul-Hamid's reign began with a cruel war with Russia and saw the loss of Cyprus and Egypt to Great Britain and of Tunisia to France soon after. Worse still, the non-Turkish peoples of the empire — Arabs, Armenians, Macedonians, and others — were agitating for independence or home-rule with varying degrees of intensity. To cope with these disruptive forces, the sultan had at his disposal a rather ineffective bureaucracy and an army that was slow to modernize. No lesser a liability was the empty State Treasury, which placed the Ottoman Empire at the mercy of international loans and prevented the implementation of reform.

It is no small tribute to Abdul-Hamid that under these circumstances he succeeded in maintaining himself on the throne for so many years. His stability was partly due to the rivalries between the European Powers, each of which jealously followed the others' activities in order to increase its own respective influence. Apparently, the Powers could agree even less about an eventual partition of the Ottoman Empire. But the sultan's success can be attributed no less to his acumen and authoritarianism.

Abdul-Hamid was a Muslim who ably exploited Pan-Islam to further his political aims. But he was not impervious to change and modernization, and he encouraged some progress in educational and judicial reforms, as well as modernization in communications and the military. These programs, however, were advanced mainly to suit his own purposes: the reforms were meant to impress the Liberals in Europe; the modernization to tighten his personal hold over the empire.

His real control, however, was ensured by a network of police agents and informers who reported directly to the sultan's office. This network was so wide that one tourist to Istanbul reported that one-half of the capital's inhabitants was busy spying on the other! Dangerous elements were dealt with ruthlessly, and the executions, exiles, and jail terms were well publicized in the press, over which a close censorship was imposed. Not unexpectedly, the paranoiac sultan became one of the most cordially hated men in the empire. He was perceptive enough to sense this hostility and lived in constant fear for his life. He hardly ever left his palaces, except to move from one to the other, or occasionally to attend the Friday noon prayer under heavy guard. However, Abdul-Hamid had an insatiable curiosity about what was going on in the empire, and he found ways to get information without risking an assassin's bullet.

One obvious means was photographs. Earlier sketches or paintings were available, but they were not always accurate and sometimes were totally unreliable. In the mid-nineteenth century, however, photography arrived in the area, and by the 1880s it had reached a high technical level of accuracy and sensitivity. So the best photographers in the empire and abroad supplied the sultan with the finest photographs they could produce, set in beautifully bound and decorated albums. Our collection is a sample of their work on Palestine.

Most of the photographers in Abdul-Hamid's empire — and certainly the best — were Christians: Armenians, Greeks, Frenchmen, Americans, and others. Perhaps this was because of the ban on registering live images common to both Judaism and Islam. The albums presented to the sultan comprised thousands of black-and-white photographs of remarkable quality. As a rule, they were offered with a humble, congratulatory letter. Fortunately, Abdul-Hamid's collection has survived in the library of the Yildiz Kiosk Palace, incorporated into the library of the University of Istanbul, and the following is a sample of the most interesting photographs of Palestine taken almost a century ago — that is, before the process of social, economic, and political change had entered into full swing.

The photographs in this volume have been selected first for their high quality and their uniqueness. To the best of my knowledge, most appear here for the first time. Secondly, I have concentrated on photographs which present views, sites, institutions, and street scenes that have changed or even disappeared altogether. Finally, preference has been given to photographs which have an evocative appeal for the history-minded and a lasting value for lovers of nature and art. Among the subjects of the photographs are views of towns, villages, and Bedouin encampments; holy places and historical sites; administrative buildings, post offices, schools, hospitals, fortresses, *caravanserais,* railway stations, bridges, harbors, and *sebils* for the thirsty traveler; bazaars and other street scenes; the visit of Kaiser Wilhelm II to Palestine; and a collection of types of people, with their particular garb, wares, and implements, such as Bedouin, peasants, boatmen, bakers, peddlers, merchants and cobblers, as well as representatives of various religious groups — the Jews, Muslims, Druze, and Christians. The photos have been arranged first geographically and then by subject: holy places and people and professions.

Palestine was conquered by the Ottoman Turks in 1516–17. In Abdul-Hamid's days — the last quarter of the nineteenth century — it was small in area and sparse in population (as we know from the very skimpy demographic statistics available), when compared with the far-flung empire that extended from North Africa to the frontiers of Iran and from the shores of the Black Sea to southern Arabia. When Abdul-Hamid II ascended the throne in 1876, Palestine was a poor, neglected part of the empire. It lacked a single developed harbor, had no railroad, and hardly any carriage roads. The population was plagued by exaggerated taxation and insecurity caused by Bedouin raids and enjoyed very few amenities and comforts.

Still, Palestine was an important part of the empire as the only land bridge between Turkey proper and North Africa, as well as the regular staging area for campaigns against the mutinous tribes in the Arabian Peninsula. Likewise, it was in many respects a fascinating country for those who resided in it; for those who came to settle — like the German Templers and the Jews who came to pray, or to settle on the land and be rejuvenated; and for the casual or observant tourist. In 1876 Palestine's population was only 400,000 and in 1895 approximately 450,000. In its heterogeneity, however, it was a microcosm of the empire. People of various

9

creeds and classes lived side by side, sometimes in the most cordial of relations, at others in angry conflicts of belief or clashes of interests. For this was an era of increasing contact between the local population and visitors from abroad: pilgrims attracted by the religious appeal of the country; businessmen interested in commerce; tourists drawn by the lure of the East; or agents furthering the interests of the European Powers in the area.

It took quite a while for these contacts to have an impact on the local population, for perhaps the most easily discernible characteristic of life in nineteenth-century Palestine was change-resistant conservatism. All the villages and Bedouin tribes and most of the towns were cut off from events in the Ottoman Empire and the world at large, since the roads were inadequate and the communications facilities virtually inaccessible. Except in Jerusalem and some other large population centers, few read newspapers, as illiteracy was widespread and abject poverty compelled almost everyone to invest his energy solely in making a living. This meant defraying the most urgent expenses of food and lodging, while paying heavy taxes and meeting the deadlines of high-interest debts.

Illness was prevalent, epidemics (such as cholera or smallpox) were not unknown, and eye diseases were rampant. Local healers usually aggravated the conditions of their patients, while qualified physicians—missionaries and others—could not always cope with the prejudice that bedeviled their work. The vicious cycle of isolation, ignorance, poverty, and disease strengthened conservatism further. In terms of material culture, this attitude was expressed in resistance to the renewal of equipment or apparel, which was never willingly discarded until hopelessly worn—and then the new purchase was a repeat of the discarded article. Once again, this was merely symptomatic of an almost general antipathy, or apathy, to innovation.

The seeds of change were sown in the generation of Abdul-Hamid's reign. They found fertile ground and sprouted after the First World War in the modernization of Palestine. Some innovations, like those in communications, were quietly absorbed by the masses. To others—whether new machinery, imported articles, improvements in agriculture and industry, education, or patterns of social behavior—there was greater resistance. And because the old coexisted with the new, tensions increased whenever the two converged.

In the second half of the nineteenth century, shipping companies increasingly included Palestine's ports in their itineraries. The last

quarter of the century saw the building of better roads between the main centers of population. The first road suitable for carriages was completed between Jaffa and Jerusalem in 1869. Later, in about 1876 — the year of Abdul-Hamid's accession to the throne — public transportation in the form of a diligence (horse-carriage) service was inaugurated on the Jaffa–Jerusalem road. Similarly, public carriage service was introduced at that time in Jerusalem — parallel with the construction of several quarters in the New City whose residents required inexpensive means of transportation — while private carriages continued to cater to the rich and the tourist trade. At about the same time, the German Templers in Haifa introduced a public carriage service between Haifa and Acre, which cut down the traveling time of four hours, on donkeys, to an hour and a quarter. A little later, they organized similar services from Haifa to Nazareth and then to Tiberias — improving the roads, at their own cost, in the process. In 1881 the Ottoman authorities initiated work on new, better roads between Jerusalem and both Hebron and Nablus.

The railroads, which covered only several hundred miles when Abdul-Hamid ascended to the throne, were developed considerably. All were constructed by European companies using foreign capital (with the exception of the Hejaz Railway, built with Ottoman funds and labor). This development further increased comfort and saved time. When the railroad from Jaffa to Jerusalem was completed in 1892, the trip by train, though only scheduled once a day in each direction, took only four hours, as compared to twelve by diligence and a whole day by mule. In 1905 another railroad line was built from Haifa to the east of the country, which linked Der'a, Transjordan, with the Hejaz Railway going north to Damascus and south to Medina; and later yet another line was laid from Haifa to Acre. This made Haifa into a major center for both the Muslim pilgrimage to Mecca and for the grain exports that were brought to the city's port from the fertile plain of Horan (Hawran) in Syria. Since foreign investments had to be protected, the authorities were careful to ensure the security of all passengers — with the assistance of both a police force and an irregular cavalry. Speedier communication therefore meant safer travel as well, and brigandage decreased proportionately, at least on the main routes.

Starting in 1854, foreign postal services — run by the French, British, Russians, Austro-Hungarians, Italians, and Germans — functioned side by side with the Ottoman system and issued their own stamps by official permission. The consuls of these states, stationed in Jerusalem, and the vice-consuls, in Jaffa and Haifa, encouraged the use of their respective postal services for both economic and political reasons. The Ottoman authorities, not insensitive to rivalry, limited the foreign postal services to these three towns for a while and opened their own offices in them, as well as elsewhere. The sacks of mail were transported to Jaffa under guard and from there were sent on each country's ships. The Ottomans permitted the railways to be used for Turkish mails alone. The same dichotomy existed in the telegraph services, the first of which was inaugurated in Jerusalem in 1860. Telegrams in Turkish and Arabic could be sent only through the Ottoman telegraph offices, while those in other languages could be presented at the foreign ones alone.

The coexistence of the different systems was also evident in the plurality of calendars (Hijri — Muslim, Financial — Ottoman, Jewish, Gregorian, Julian), weights and measures, and more particularly in the currency in use. The increase in tourism and pilgrimages during Abdul-Hamid's reign brought a considerable flow of money into Palestine. Incidentally, it also caused a marked rise in prices and brought about a situation whereby the currencies of all major countries were generally accepted by the local people. In addition to Ottoman money, English, French, Austro-Hungarian, and Russian coins were frequently used. Paper money, however, was virtually unknown and often refused, especially in the villages. Indeed, the Ottoman government introduced paper money for the first time during the Russo-Turkish War of 1877-78 but later had to withdraw it, due to its rejection by a suspicious public. Concurrently, in many of the rural villages, small coins were frequently difficult to procure, so that the local people bartered their own produce against what they bought in the village shop.

Life was changing imperceptibly, and by the turn of the century, as Abdul-Hamid's reign was drawing to its close, some of the details of change began to be noticeable, especially in the larger population centers. Food and drink became more varied. White bread, rarely eaten before, became more common. While water, milk, and coffee had been consumed for generations, tea (formerly restricted to the Turkish officials) was introduced by East European Jews. New household utensils and better furniture, such as beds, were slowly introduced. New fashions in clothes were increasingly imported, and a larger number of local inhabitants began to wear shoes regularly. Kerosene was brought from Batum (in Russia) and Rumania; in Abdul-Hamid's days it was in almost universal use in urban areas, while candles and lamps were preferred in rural parts.

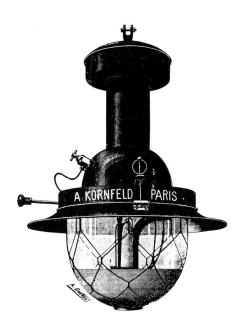

Still, since Palestine's economy during the nineteenth century was based chiefly on subsistence agriculture, in towns and cities almost as much as in the villages, even the urban or semi-urban population had to rely largely on the agricultural lands adjoining their town for their food supply. The cities and towns served as marketplaces for the rural areas in the vicinity; but the edges of the towns preserved a semi-rural character. Even Jerusalem, beyond the city walls, contained sizable farms.

Palestine's urban centers were small in size and population, towns rather than cities. Jerusalem, the only one which could claim to be a city, had over 20,000 inhabitants at the time of Abdul-Hamid's accession; Gaza, the second largest city, had 16,000; and Nablus was approaching the 12,000 mark. All the others had less than 10,000 people at the time. Limited though they were, the towns were large enough to enable the members of various religious communities to live together, by their own choice, in what were actually separate — although not insulated — quarters. Security considerations (especially for the minority groups), no less than religious practices and, possibly, natural inclination, were factors. Indeed, in some cases each quarter had its own solid-iron gates, which were closed and locked at night and in times of danger. More than any other physical sign, the walls and gates of each quarter highlighted the isolation of each religious community from the others. There was no common feeling for the town, and the elders of a community, or the representatives of a professional group, guarded their respective interests by direct negotiation with the Ottoman authorities. Since the governmental structure was complex and proliferated among numerous organs, relations with the authorities were a complicated affair. The Provincial Municipalities Law of 1877, which aimed at decentralization and some popular representation, was important in its conception, but changed little in actual practice.

Jerusalem excepted, there was little of architectural interest in the urban private homes. Many houses in the towns were of the primitive village type, with flat roofs. Those of the well to do varied in size, but variations from the plain square walls were rare. In the interior, arches added to the beauty that was all too often lacking on the outside. The streets were generally narrow, winding, and dusty, with only the central arteries being paved. They were often dirty, as the sanitary services were sparsely manned and poorly equipped (indeed, the inadequacy of sanitation was highlighted by the population increase). Most streets were dark at night, or at best dimly lit by paraffin-oil lamps, and consequently dangerous.

Nevertheless, there was an immense difference in quality between village or Bedouin and town life. Not surprisingly, it was the dream of many peasants to move to town, for the urban centers had, among other attractions, schools—at least for the lucky ones, which at the time still meant boys alone. The opportunities to an education in late nineteenth-century Palestine were greater for the Jews and Christians than for the Muslims and Druze, because the former were more ready to organize and finance the schooling by themselves. Although the government made a determined effort to encourage education among the Muslims in the later years of Abdul-Hamid's reign, it lacked the initiative and the funds to achieve concrete progress.

The trades were usually grouped in separate streets in the Palestinian town. Practically all the shoemakers, for instance, were nextdoor neighbors, while the clothdealers or the fruiterers had their own bazaars. Most shops were a one-room establishment where all the merchandise was stacked rather than displayed; when there was a second room, it was generally used for storage. As a rule, workshops were also small; but considering the relatively primitive character of the tools, the quality of the finished products—in carpentry, for example—was often surprisingly good. Shops and workshops were open and engaged in business from some time after sunrise until sunset. Time was of no great consequence, and much of it was invested in haggling, which usually followed a pattern and was looked upon as a sort of sport.

The peasants, Bedouin, and many townspeople displayed conservative tastes, sticking to the same goods that had pleased their parents and grandparents, with only the color allowing for variations in taste. Conformity to generally accepted tastes was the rule. For instance, Oriental cloth and brass goods brought down from Damascus found almost universal favor. Gradually, however, in the latter part of Abdul-Hamid's reign, the more affluent and more susceptible to change among the townspeople—generally the Christians—increasingly patronized shops that provided European prints, French silks and parasols, and high-healed satin slippers generally imported via Beirut. At the same time, restaurants and coffee houses of a better quality were opened in such towns as Jerusalem and Haifa.

The Arab villages were smaller than the towns and even more isolated from the rest of the world, particularly if they lay off the beaten track. This was frequently the case in Palestine, where many villages were constructed on the top or side of a hill for reasons of security. The houses were poorer than in town, smaller (generally, one story high), built closer to one another, and frequently windowless. Even the more affluent, who built two-story homes of stone, abstained from making their exterior too attractive,

for fear of awakening the rapacity of the authorities and tax collectors. The subsistence economy was even more pronounced in the village than in the town and was largely based on agriculture and the raising of sheep, goats and cattle. Since many peasants, probably most, lacked the funds to tide them over a bad harvest, to buy oxen, or to buy and repair their implements, they sank into debt and became even poorer than before. Indeed, whatever modest services they could afford had to be paid for in kind. Thus the barber, who came at infrequent intervals to cut the men's hair (no such service was provided for the women), received his fee in agricultural produce, as did the peddler who came to sell inexpensive cloth.

The isolation of the village and the unchanging rhythm of its life hardly seemed to bother the villagers, whose almost universal illiteracy was not conducive to higher expectations. Deeply religious and rather superstitious, as a rule, the villager was generally not a hard worker or troubled by close living quarters, lack of furniture, simple food, and dreary clothes, provided his life was anchored in relative tranquility among objects with which he was familiar and within a framework of social relations to which he was accustomed. He was not really bothered by the lack of privacy — the fact that in the village anybody might walk into a house at almost any time, join the conversation, and seek or impart information without reservation. This behavior is at least partly explained by kinship: in many villages, all the inhabitants were part of an enlarged family or, in the larger villages, members of the several families living there. Actually, most of the social relations and the economic practices were decided upon in the context of the family unit, with the head of the family (or enlarged family) responsible for the decisions. He would consult with his wife or wives in matters concerning the marrying off of their children. Incidentally, the Arab villager of Palestine in the late nineteenth century was much more monogamous than is generally thought. The Jews and Christians obviously took only one wife, and the Muslims could hardly afford to pay the bride-price more than once (and even that one time was difficult).

The Bedouin vied with the peasants in poverty. Once the prototype of the nomad, they were gradually changing some of their patterns of life during Abdul-Hamid's era, at least in parts of Palestine west of the Jordan River, that is, farther away from the desert. Quite a few were displaying signs of semi-sedentarization, particularly in their pursuit of agriculture on land they had seized or leased. The mainstay of the Bedouin economy, however, continued to be the raising of sheep (mainly in southern Palestine) and goats (chiefly in Galilee), and they bought their needs with money obtained from the sale of sheep, camels, horses, donkeys, and handiwork.

Another important source of income for the Bedouin was their constant raiding of villages (sometimes even of towns) and the waylaying of travelers. Since the police forces, even with military assistance, could not subdue them permanently, the Ottoman authorities bought off the strongest and most aggressive tribes. In time, the tribes came to expect these payments, which were institutionalized in all but name as an annual tribute. The practice was more common in the area east of the Jordan River than west of it. However, with the improvement in the carriage roads and the increase of traffic on them, and most particularly with the expansion of the railroad network and the increase in the armed protection offered it by the authorities, the opportunities for Bedouin harassment decreased. This change occurred especially in northern Palestine, where Bedouin attacks became rare, while in the south and east of the Jordan, they declined in frequency.

Bedouin life at the time still followed the rules dictated by a sparse existence in a hostile environment—and these rules were obeyed even by those who had become semi-sedentarized. As with the peasants, kinship was considered all-important. The sheikh of the tribe had a very marked sway over its members. However, even he was limited by the hallowed customs governing Bedouin life. The Bedouin are all Muslims, and accepted tradition (bolstered by superstition) dictated living in tents, roaming about in the wilderness, providing hospitality, the seeking of refuge, and blood feuds, as well as many details involved in grinding coffee, the partaking of food, and the manner of dress and of fighting. The women shared the hardships of a tough life with their men. Most Bedouin, their sheikhs excepted, were monogamous, for, like the peasants, they could not afford to pay for more than one bride. In addition, their way of life was hardly conducive to maintaining more than one household—and experience had obviously taught them what it meant to keep more than one wife in a Bedouin tent.

The changes in Abdul-Hamid's Palestine were reflected in all walks of life among the country's social groups. The overall population increased through immigration and rising tourism, though, unfortunately, no reliable figures are available and the estimates vary widely from one another. The religious communities also played a role in this growth. The Muslims, apparently the least inclined to change, grew in numbers through both natural increase and the drafting by the Ottoman authorities of non-Arab Muslims formerly living beyond Palestine. The best known among these ethnic groups were the Circassians, who had been driven out of the Caucasus by Russian colonization and were settled by the Ottoman authorities in Galilee and in garrisons on the edge of the desert east of the Jordan; and the Bosnians, who sought refuge after the Austrians snatched Bosnia from the Ottoman Empire in 1877 and were settled near Caesarea. The Christians, split into many denominations, absorbed additional numbers from among the missionaries and German Templers, thus increasing their contacts with Europe.

But it was the Jews, so it seems, who provided the strongest impetus to modernization in the era of Abdul-Hamid. Arriving in more substantial numbers from 1882 on, chiefly from Europe, the Jews had a very real impact on the village and town—bringing with them ways related to their European experience. While some of them joined the local urban communities in their orthodox quarters in the four holy cities (Jerusalem, Hebron, Tiberias, and Safed), others contributed to innovation. They introduced modern agriculture into their settlements, adopted newer methods, and were advised by the agricultural school established at Mikveh Israel in 1870. In the towns—where most of the Jews resided — they improved the banking system and promoted local and foreign commerce. They had a larger share than is generally suspected in the manual trades, but left a more lasting mark on the transition from traditional methods to modern technology. For instance, they tried a new sort of iron plow (instead of the wooden one); founded a modern metal factory (1888), glass factory (1894), perfume plant (in the 1890s), and weaving plant for the silk industry (about 1900); and promoted modern wine production.

Not less relevant, the Jews of Palestine, who were distinguished by a high percentage of literacy, made a noticeable contribution to culture. Of course, all communities, though not to an identical degree, continued the study and promotion of their respective religions, as was only natural to, and typical of, the Holy Land. But the Jews also had an important share in the introduction of secular schools and the publication of a secular press. In the early 1840s, the first Hebrew printing press was introduced in Jerusalem. By the turn of the century, the Jews owned ten printing presses, out of a total of eighteen in the city. In 1863 the monthly *Ha-Levanon* ("The Lebanon") began publication, followed five months later by another periodical, *Ha-Havatzelet* ("The Lily"), and soon followed by several others. In other words, the only periodicals of a non-religious nature published in the late nineteenth century were in Hebrew, and they contained a good proportion of news and features about the outside world. *Al-Karmil* ("The Carmel"), the first regular secular Arab periodical in Palestine, appeared in Haifa only in 1909—that is, right at the close of the period under discussion. Thus it was the Hebrew press which both reflected and contributed to the change in Abdul-Hamid's Palestine.

HORAN

TRANSJORDAN

Der'a

As-Salt

MOAB

Ghoraniyya
Bridge

Jordan River

Dead Sea

Sea of
Galilee

Capernaum

Tiberias

Jericho

Nebi Musa

St. George Convent

Mar Saba Convent

Safed

Al-Khan al-Ahmar

'Azariyya (St Lazarus Tom

Mt. Tabor

Kafr Kana

Jerusalem

Silwan

Nazareth

Mt. Ebal

Jenin Nablus

Plateau of Mitzpa

Bethlehem

GALILEE

Samaria

Beth-El

JUDEAN HILLS

Mt. Gerizim

Abu-Ghosh

Hebron

Acre

Mt. Carmel

Latrun

Bab-el-Wad

Haifa

Lod

Ramle

Caesarea

Mikveh Israel

Jaffa

Yibne

E

N

S

W

Mediterranean Sea

Gaza

18

PALESTINE at the Time of ABDUL-HAMID II
LATE 19th CENTURY

erak

Petra

Akaba

Red Sea

Note: Map shows place names mentioned in text

| 0 | 10 | 20 Miles |
| 0 | 10 | 20 | 30 Kms |

19

Jaffa

Jaffa is an ancient port and played an important role in Jewish history during the Second Temple period (516 B.C.E. — 70 C.E.). It was a comparatively large town boasting a commercial harbor during the Roman and Byzantinian periods and was small but still commercially active during the era of Arab rule, from the mid-seventh century. Jaffa's importance rose considerably during the Crusader period, as it was one of the ports connecting the Holy Land with Europe, but the town was conquered and partly destroyed by Saladin in 1187 and was neglected by the Mameluke and early Ottoman rulers. Only from the late seventeenth century on did the town begin to rise in standing. The turning point came in the early nineteenth century, when Abu Nabbut Mehmet Pasha, the Turkish governor who ruled Jaffa from 1810 to 1820, restored some of its former status. He rebuilt its walls and endowed it with public buildings, including a large mosque. He also built two beautiful *sebils,* fountains for the weary traveler: one in Jaffa, the other on the way leading to Jerusalem, about half a mile from Jaffa's eastern gate.

Jaffa was rebuilt after the 1837 earthquake. During the nineteenth century — like the ports of Gaza, Haifa and Acre — it suffered from the competitively rapid development of Beirut; but Jaffa continued to advance. Progress was slow, yet from the mid-nineteenth century there was an improvement in sanitation and some streets were paved. In the 1860s more new houses were built, shipping agencies were opened, a lighthouse was erected, and telegraph lines were put up.

The *sebil* of Abu Nabbut Mehmet Pasha, about half a mile from Jaffa's eastern gate on the main road to Jerusalem. The fountain was built for thirsty travelers by the above governor of Jaffa (1810-1820) as a philanthropic gesture. The governor himself is said to be buried nearby

overleaf
General view of Jaffa and its harbor

In the era of Abdul-Hamid, many Jaffa residents still lived off the groves of oranges, lemons, and pomegranates, as well as the plentiful fruit, in the town's environs. Increasingly, however, they gravitated toward business connected with the port. Jaffa traded with Egypt, Syria, and Turkey; its chief exports were oranges,

wheat, soap, and sesame. For many years its harbor remained the chief gateway to Abdul-Hamid's Palestine. Most of the trips to Jerusalem began there and went on via Ramle and Bab al-Wad, at the foot of the Judean Hills, especially after the road from Jaffa to Jerusalem was improved to serve carriage traffic in the late 1860s and the Jaffa–Ramle–Jerusalem railroad was inaugurated in 1892. Nevertheless, travelers often complained of the service in the port. Rocks prevented the ships from approaching the shore. Passengers and luggage were lowered into boats, unless the weather was rough — in which case the ship had to proceed to Haifa or Beirut. A guidebook of the period remarked, "The debarcation at Jaffa . . . is invariably conducted with the least possible order and the greatest possible noise." In theory, passports with a Turkish visa were required of all travelers, but a visiting card and *baksheesh* were said to suffice as well. People were searched not only on arrival but also on departure, to prevent the smuggling of antiquities.

While estimates of Jaffa's population conflict, one may assume that

The customs house of Jaffa. In the late nineteenth century, close to 40 percent of all the customs dues collected in Palestine were taken in here.

The St. Louis French Hospital, not far from the seashore

The St. Luke's Scottish Mission and School

The police station and jail house, near the seashore

The English Hospital of the Church Missionary Society, near St. Luke's (today a center for mental-health care)

on Abdul-Hamid's accession in 1876 it was around 8,000, with the Muslims accounting for the majority. Along with Haifa, Jaffa was one of the fastest growing towns. Ten years later it had doubled its population to about 17,000; in 1897 it reached approximately the 35,000 mark; and toward the end of Abdul-Hamid's reign, in 1908,

Mikveh Israel, near Jaffa, soon after it had been established by Charles Netter in 1870 as an agricultural school. Its importance can be gauged when one remembers that at the end of the century there were more than 5,000 Jews in Palestine's agricultural settlements, using more advanced methods than those employed in the rest of the Ottoman Empire

The Jaffa railway station, inaugurated in 1892

it was said to be close to 50,000. Not a few of these inhabitants were Jews, some of whom were in the process of leaving old Jaffa to settle in new quarters on its periphery. A few of these were living in Mikveh Israel, where a new agricultural school had been set up in 1870 on the initiative of French Jewry.

Ramle and Lod

Ramle is the only town in Palestine founded by the Arabs. Popular etymology explains that its name is derived from the Arabic *raml* ("sand"). It was built around 716 C.E. by the Umayyad caliph Ibn 'Abd al-Malik on a site controlling the main route from Damascus to Cairo. Ramle was the capital of the country from its foundation until the Crusader period. A coin mint was set up there soon after the town was established, which attests to Ramle's importance. In later years, it served mainly as a stopover for Christian pilgrims riding from Jaffa to Jerusalem. Despite the heavy damage it suffered in early Ottoman times as a result of the earthquake of 1546, Ramle continued to host Christian pilgrims and served as the center of an administrative unit in Ottoman Palestine. Its population at the beginning of Abdul-Hamid's reign was approximately 3,000, of whom about two-thirds were Muslims and one-third Christians (mainly Greeks and Armenians), along with a few Jews.

Lod (Lydda) is an ancient city, dating from the Second Temple period. It was Ramle's neighbor and chief rival, and there existed an almost constant see-saw relationship between them, as one's rise inevitably meant the other's decline. Indeed, Lod's downward trend began with the foundation of Ramle. It had its heyday in the Crusader period, when it was an important center, overshadowing Ramle. Lod's Church of St. George, in the possession of the Greek-Orthodox Church in Abdul-Hamid's days, remained an important landmark, although it was partly in ruins. At the time, Lod's population reached between 1,500 and 2,000 souls.

The inhabitants of both Ramle and Lod lived off agriculture, some primitive soap production, and the tourist trade. The most common route from Jaffa to Jerusalem passed via Ramle, particularly after a special carriage road had been built in the late 1860s. The carriages used to leave Jaffa in the afternoon and reached Ramle, where the travelers rested, visited Ramle and Lod, and then

The Tower of Ramle, part of a larger edifice, al-Jami' al-Abyad ("The White Mosque"), built in the eighth century C.E. and restored by Saladin. The present tower is a minaret dating from the fourteenth century. During the British Mandate, its picture was to adorn the 5-pound banknote

overleaf
General view of Ramle with the town's cemetery in the foreground

The *khan* (*caravanserai*) in Bab al-Wad, on the main road from Ramle to Jerusalem

General view of Lod (Lydda). To the left are the old mosque and its minaret, and on their right the Church of St. George and some ruins, probably from Crusader times

below
A *sebil* in Ramle set in the wall of a Crusader church turned into a mosque

proceeded to the *caravanserai* (the *khan*) at Bab al-Wad, a two-story inn built by the Municipality of Jerusalem. There most travelers spent the night on the second floor, while their horses were rested and fed in the stables on the first. The authorities collected a road tax on all carriages. With the inauguration of the Jaffa–Ramle–Jerusalem railroad in 1892, Ramle's importance increased still further.

Jerusalem

Jerusalem, Palestine's largest city — actually, the only population center deserving of the name—was a typical mountain city in Abdul-Hamid's time. Jews, Christians, and Muslims have considered it as a holy city and accorded it a special place in their tradition; both Jewish and Christian legend had it that Jerusalem was the center of the world. Sultan Selim I conquered Jerusalem in 1516-17, and Süleyman the Magnificent (1520-1566) built the handsome wall around its Old City measuring about 2.5 miles (4 kms.). Constructed entirely of stone — some of its components pre-date the Ottoman conquest — it has remained one of the few complete city walls in the area of the empire. Like the wall, most of the Turkish construction work dates from the early period of Ottoman rule, when the Citadel was repaired, a camp for the garrison was established, and the Sultan's Pool was built outside the Old City and below the wall.

Most of the holy places in Jerusalem were situated in the Old City or near it. The heaviest concentration was on Mount Moriah, which covered close to one-fifth of the entire surface of the Old City. Most of the provincial Ottoman administration was located in the Old City, including the telegraph office and postal services. It was also the residence of the *wali,* or governor. The *majlis,* or Town Council, managed municipal affairs. At the time of Abdul-Hamid's accession, this council consisted of four Muslims, three Christians and one Jew. It was one of the few bureaucratic levels of encounter between members of the various religious communities. Barring business contacts and a small degree of social intercourse, however, these communities led separate religious and cultural lives in their respective Old City quarters, of which the Muslim Quarter was the largest.

Cramped for space in the 1850s and 1860s, the Jews and several Christian denominations began to buy lands beyond the Old City wall (despite the difficulties raised by the Ottoman bureaucracy),

A street leading from St. Stephen's Gate to the Via Dolorosa. On the right are the ruins of the tower of the al-Mu'azzamiyya School, a Muslim College built in 1218 C.E. The tower itself was built about fifty years later

left
The religious ceremony inaugurating the railway station in Jerusalem on September 26, 1892. The Jaffa–Jerusalem railroad was an exciting innovation and heralded better and safer transport

right
The Old City viewed from the northeast. The Dome of the Rock is prominent in the background

overleaf
View of Jerusalem from Mount Scopus

below
General view of Jerusalem

left above
The Mount of Olives (upper right) and Gethsemane (center). The Mount of Olives served in Abdul-Hamid's time largely as a cemetery for Jews, who considered burial there as highly meritorious

left below
Birket as-Sultan ("The Pool of the Sultan") was the site of an ancient pool restored by Süleyman the Magnificent in 1536. It was situated between Mount Zion and the Old City wall in the east (right) and Mishkenot Sha'ananim, the first Jewish quarter in the New City, in the west. The road from Jerusalem to Bethlehem — seen clearly in the photograph — passed over a dam

right, above & center:
Outside the Jaffa Gate (or Bab al-Khalil, "The Hebron Gate"). While all the other gates were regularly closed after sunset, the Jaffa Gate remained open and all traffic passed through it, supervised by the nearby garrison. To its west was the starting point of the carriage route to Jaffa; to its south the route to Bethlehem and Hebron

right, below
Inside the Jaffa Gate. This was a center of business and public life, as it was close to the government offices and the Municipality. The building on the left was the Austro-Hungarian post office

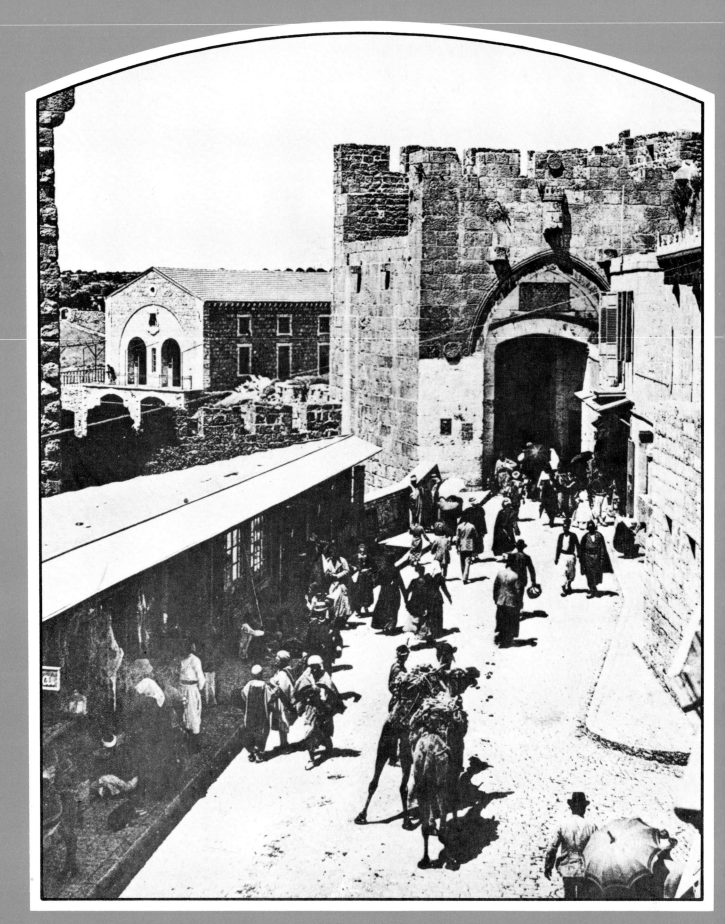

left
Inside the Jaffa Gate. The small
building on the left and the adjoining
part of the Old City wall were brought
down to allow Kaiser Wilhelm of
Germany to enter riding on his steed in
October 1898. They were never
rebuilt

right, above, below
The Tower of David, built of very
large stones, some reaching 10 feet in
length. The Ottoman flag at the top is a
reminder that the tower and its area
were garrisoned by the Turks
throughout Abdul-Hamid's reign

opposite
The Armenian Convent Mar Ya'kub (St. Jacques) in the Armenian Quarter within the Old City wall

right
The *sebil* of Kaytbay (a Mameluke sultan), built in 1482 to the west of the Dome of the Rock. To its left is the spout, built by Kasim Pasha in 1527, for washing one's hands and feet before prayer

below
The Pool of Hezekiah, viewed from the south, in the Christian Quarter of the Old City. In the background are the two domes of the Church of the Holy Sepulchre

The Damascus Gate to the Old City. Built — or restored — by Süleyman the Magnificent, this is a fine example of sixteenth-century architecture. The gate proper consists of two gate towers. On each side are very slender columns, which have given the gate its Arabic name, Bab al-'Amud ("Gate of the Column")

and constructed homes and public buildings, such as schools, hospitals, and hostels. These were built, as a rule, in Jerusalem stone. The workers were chiefly Arabs from Bethlehem, which boasted good stonemasons; somewhat later, Jews also started to work in construction. The new buildings were not far from the wall and were generally on main traffic arteries — between the Jaffa and Damascus Gates and along (or near) Jaffa Road. Small shops were opened in modest houses on both sides of Jaffa Road, one side being Jewish, the other Christian.

In 1855, ground was broken for the Jewish Quarter of Mishkenot Sha'ananim, opposite Mount Zion and across from the Pool of the Sultan. In the same year, Father J.L. Schneller purchased a large plot that was to serve for the construction of an Evangelical school for orphan boys. In about 1860 the Russian-Orthodox Church bought a large plot near Jaffa Road and began building a Russian Compound for its consulate, cathedral, and a large hostel (comprising 1,000 beds) for its pilgrims. In this way the Jews, the Russian-Orthodox Cathedral, the German Evangelical Church, the

The Ma'muniyya State Primary School in the Muslim Quarter of the Old City, north of the Dome of the Rock, which is seen in the right background (today it is named the Kadisiyya School)

The Ethiopian Church during its construction in 1887 outside the walls of the Old City in what came to be known as the Ethiopian Quarter

The French Hospital of the St. Louis Convent (later, Notre Dame), erected in 1887 outside and facing the Old City wall. It was built and maintained by a French order, Les Pères Augustins de l'Assomption

Guest house of the St. Louis Convent. The photograph is of the west side, that is, the back of the building facing the Old City wall

top, left
The Meyer Rothschild Jewish Hospital, located between the Ethiopian Church and the Russian Compound (today part of the Seligsberg Vocational School)

top, right
The Jewish vocational school near the corner of Jaffa Road and the Street of the Consuls (later renamed Street of the Prophets)

French Catholics, and some others shared between them the privilege of setting up the New City of Jerusalem. The German Templers settled in the Rephaim Quarter soon afterward. American missionaries, Armenians, Greeks, and others followed to the New City. By the time Abdul-Hamid mounted the throne, the building of various quarters of the New City had already begun. However, it was mainly during his reign that the New City grew and a sizable part of the commerce, workshops, and services moved from the Old City into the New.

left
The Russian Cathedral in Jerusalem, centerpiece of the Russian Compound, was built—with a special *ferman* ("permit") of the sultan—between 1860 and 1864 and is richly decorated in its interior

opposite
Yad Absalom, in the Valley of Jehoshaphat. Although probably dating from the Greco-Roman period, the tomb was thought by many Jews to be that of Absalom, who had rebelled against his father, King David. In Abdul-Hamid's era, the Jews still used to pelt this monument with stones, as a sign of their repugnance for filial disobedience

below
St. Paul's Evangelical Church, built outside the Old City walls in 1873

The Valley of Jehoshaphat, containing part of the Jewish cemetery on the adjacent Mount of Olives. Many considered it a great privilege to be buried here, particularly near the tomb attributed to the Prophet Zechariah (in the right foreground), hewn entirely out of the rock. In the left foreground is a cave with an inscription saying that in it were housed the tombs of the Bene Hizir, a priestly family in the First Temple era

The Plateau of Mitzpa, or Nebi Samu'il, where Arab legend has it that Samuel was buried. In Abdul-Hamid's days, the village consisted of an old mosque and a few inhabited houses

The visit of Kaiser Wilhelm II of Germany in October–November 1898, centering on Jerusalem, was undoubtedly the showiest event in the country during Abdul-Hamid's reign, and was long remembered as such. With an escort of two hundred, the Kaiser landed in Haifa, visited Jaffa, then rode to Jerusalem via Ramle, Latrun, and Abu Ghosh. He spent a whole week in Jerusalem, with a side trip to Bethlehem — all accompanied by great pomp, speeches, and celebrations. The ceremonial deference of the Ottoman authorities lent an added aura to this unusual visit.

The triumphant procession of Kaiser Wilhelm and his escort in Jerusalem, 1898. The streets were bedecked in his honor, and special arches were set up

While the various sources offer conflicting estimates regarding the size of Jerusalem's population, they all agree that it increased rapidly in Abdul-Hamid's reign. Numbering just a few thousand inhabitants in the first third of the nineteenth century, the city had some 25,000 on this sultan's accession. In 1880, it was estimated to comprise about 30,000; ten years later the figure was approximately 40,000; and at the turn of the century it passed the 45,000 mark, consisting then of 28,200 Jews, 8,700 Christians, and 8,600 Muslims.

The camp of Kaiser Wilhelm and his escort in Jerusalem. The Old City and the Mount of Olives are visible in the background

Bethlehem and Hebron

Bethlehem, the home of King David's family and the birthplace of Jesus, has always had many historical associations. It is situated 2,527 ft. (758 m.) above sea level and is about 5.5 miles (9 kms.) south of Jerusalem. In the middle of the nineteenth century, the Ottoman authorities intervened in the Christian quarrels concerning the ownership of the Church of the Nativity and determined its functional division between the denominations, laying down the rules for the order of the ritual. These rules remained unchanged until the end of Ottoman domination. In Abdul-Hamid's time, the Roman Catholics, Greeks, and Armenians had monasteries and schools; the smaller German (Protestant) community also owned a school.

The inhabitants of Bethlehem lived off agriculture, as the environs comprised fertile corn fields in the valleys and fig trees and vines on the terraces, and from the proceeds of the pilgrim and tourist trades and the sale of artifacts such as icons, crucifixes, rosaries, beads and fancy articles in olive wood, mother-of-pearl, coral, and Dead Sea stones. Bethlehem was also the marketplace for the peasants and Bedouin in the neighborhood, some of whom came to the town from as far as the Dead Sea region. Bethlehem maintained its Christian character, however. On Abdul-Hamid's accession, it had about 5,000 inhabitants, of whom only some 300 were Muslims. The population later increased substantially.

Hebron, a town dating from early biblical times, was an important Muslim center during this period. It was situated in the fertile surroundings of vines, almond trees, and apricot trees. In addition to these sources of livelihood, Hebron was famous for its manufacture of glass, and waterskins from goat hides provided yet another source of income. In addition, Bedouin came to Hebron to sell carpets and garments made of sheep hides. Hebron's

Abraham's Oak (or the "Oak of Mamre"), about 2 miles (3.5 kms.) north of Hebron, near the road to Jerusalem. An ancient tree, its picture appeared on a map dated *c.* 1300. In 1890 its girth was said to be nearly 33 feet (*c.* 10 m.)

The Greek-Orthodox Convent of Mar Elias, on the route from Jerusalem to Bethlehem. A popular legend has it that the Prophet Elijah visited the place, allegedly named after him. More likely, it seems to have been built by a Bishop Elias, was destroyed, and was then rebuilt by the Crusaders around 1160

View of Bethlehem showing a street scene

General view of Bethlehem

population grew in the nineteenth century and reached about 9,000, including approximately 500 Jews in 1876. The number of inhabitants increased later, but comprised very few Christians — only twenty-six, according to an 1895 estimate.

Peasants from the neighborhood of Bethlehem. The town's market was a natural meeting place for the peasants of the area

opposite
An Arab merchant from Bethlehem on his donkey. Buying and selling, chiefly to tourists and Christian pilgrims, was the mainstay of the town's economy

right
Kaiser Wilhelm visiting the Weihnachtskirche ("The Christmas Church") in Bethlehem on October 30, 1898

overleaf
General view of Hebron

Jericho to Akaba

The ride from Jerusalem to Jericho took about six hours. The Ottoman authorities used to farm out the right of escorting travelers to Jericho, and when Abdul-Hamid ascended the throne, this privilege had for some time been in the hands of the sheikh of Abu Dis, a Muslim village on the slopes of the Mount of Olives, near the road to Jericho.

Jericho, of biblical fame, was situated 835 feet (250 m.) below the level of the Mediterranean Sea. In the Ottoman period, it was in ruins and only sparsely inhabited. Some monks lived there, and afterward a few Bedouin and Arab peasants joined them. The place decayed further, however, and in 1871 it was almost entirely destroyed by fire. Afterward it looked even more like a village with modest houses. In 1876 Jericho was estimated to have only sixty families. At the end of the century, this number rose to about 300 families, including two Jewish merchants.

The main demographic feature of the area east of the Jordan River was the Bedouin. They roamed the territory at the edge of the desert and, although they were subsidized by the Ottoman authorities to buy a security of sorts, did not refrain from attacking and robbing travelers — even those moving in groups with an escort. Since this endangered not only the occasional foreign-tourist trade but also the more important Muslim pilgrimage route from Damascus to Medina, Ottoman troops were permanently garrisoned in strategic forts.

One of these was Kerak, in the ancient Land of Moab. On a height of 3,000 feet (900 m.) above sea level, commanding the caravan route from Syria to Egypt and Arabia, Kerak had served as a key fortress of the Nabateans and then of the Crusaders, until it was captured by Saladin in 1198. In Ottoman times, Kerak's inhabitants looked after their own affairs, trading with both the Bedouin and the

Wadi Kelt and the Mar Girius (St. George) Convent of the Greek-Orthodox Church. The wadi leads into the Jordan River

people of Hebron. At the time of Abdul-Hamid's accession, it was the administrative center of the district of Ma'an. The population of Kerak and its environs consisted of about 6,000 Muslims (including the Turkish garrison) and 1,800 Christians. Tourists repeatedly remarked that all adults carried firearms.

Another fortress was in Akaba, a station on the Damascus–Mecca pilgrimage road and a key point for navigation into the Red Sea. In Ottoman times, its only building of consequence was the fortress-castle dating from the sixteenth century.

Bethany. The Arab village of al-'Azariyya on the road leading from Jerusalem to Jericho, consisting then of about forty modest houses of Muslims only, was the site of Bethany, where Jesus brought about the resuscitation of Lazarus. The tomb of St. Lazarus is the main feature of the area and gives the village its name

top
Nebi Musa—the "Tomb of Moses"—and the mosque near it. Northwest of the Dead Sea, it was a frequent goal of pilgrimage for Muslims from near and far during Abdul-Hamid's reign

below
Al-Khan al-Ahmar ("The Red *Caravanserai*"), on the way to Jericho, so named because of the reddish coloring of its stone

The Convent of Mar Saba. Erected in
the fifth or sixth century by the Greek-
Orthodox St. Saba, this is a lofty
structure, a maze of precipices and
passages built in terraces on a
mountain side. At the time, it was
inhabited by about seventy Greek-
Orthodox monks who welcomed male
visitors provided with letters of
introduction from the authorities of
the Greek-Orthodox community in
Jerusalem—but never after sunset

left
The Russian monastery and pilgrim hostel in Jericho

opposite
The northern end of the Dead Sea

opposite
Near the mouth of the Jordan River, where it enters the Dead Sea. At that time the banks of the river were richer in foliage than nowadays

left
The Jordan Hotel near Jericho. Newly built in Abdul-Hamid's reign to cater to the tourist trade, it stood in marked contrast to the almost uninhabited area near it. At the time, Jericho was hardly more than a village

The Ghoraniyya Bridge and a gate leading to its entrance. Built over the Ghor, or Jordan River Valley, on the route from Jericho to as-Salt, it was destroyed in the First World War, and the Allenby Bridge was built in its stead

Nomad Bedouin before their tents
near the Jordan River. The size of the
tent and its quality indicated the socio-
economic status of its owner. In this
case, the tents were of the most
common and simple type, made of
dark goatskins and consequently
nicknamed by the Bedouin themselves
''Houses of Hair''

overleaf
The fortress of Kerak viewed from its
eastern side, where the wall had a
sloped, battered base. The walls were
very thick and well preserved.
Although the upper stories were in
ruins, this fortress remained an
impressive example of a Crusader
castle

opposite
The *sik* (or gorge, in Turkish), on the way to Petra, east of the Jordan

General view of Kerak, 10.5 miles (17 kms.) east of the southern tip of the Dead Sea, with the Government House in the foreground

The Government House (the *saray*) in Kerak

below
The interior of the fortress in Akaba. In Abdul-Hamid's time, Akaba was a small fishing village. Its only important building was the fortress, built by the Turks in the sixteenth century — when they conquered the area — to protect the pilgrimage route to Mecca. Its walls were very thick and, in some places, 50 feet (15 m.) high

Gaza and environs

One of the most ancient cities in the Middle East, Gaza had witnessed numerous wars, being coveted as a port on the caravan route from Syria to Egypt. Since Saladin's time (the twelfth century), it had been of relatively little importance. The Ottoman Turks captured it in 1516 on their way to conquer Egypt. Although it still played a role then, and later, as a trade center and a station on the caravan route, its economic functions decreased with the increasing Bedouin disruption of commerce on the roads leading to and from Gaza. Though similar to a large village in its general appearance, Gaza's importance grew somewhat in the nineteenth century as a seat of the Ottoman administration. By the time of Abdul-Hamid's accession, Gaza's population was second only to that of Jerusalem. It had approximately 16,000 inhabitants at the time, practically all Muslims. There were also said to be sixty-five Christian families in Gaza, mostly Greek Orthodox and a few Protestants. In 1890 there were reports of some seventy-five Jews as well.

left
The Tomb of Abu Hurayra, near the village of Yibne, was attributed to one of the companions of the Prophet Muhammad, although it is known that Abu Hurayra died and was buried in Medina

overleaf
General view of Gaza. A very ancient city, under Abdul-Hamid Gaza was still a port, though located about 2 miles (3 kms.) inland

The Jamakiyya *sebil* in Gaza

The Ottoman post office in Gaza with the telegraph lines noticeable over the left part of the building. In order to tighten his control over Palestine, Abdul-Hamid invested both efforts and funds in better communications

The building of the Municipality in Gaza

The Government House (the *saray*) in Gaza. Built in the thirteenth century, with its stones skilfully jointed, it had a rather dilapidated look by Abdul-Hamid's time. On passing the two guards, in their white jackets, at the main entrance, one came into a large courtyard where prison cells could be seen

The Rashidiyya School for Muslim children in Gaza

Interior of al-Jami' al-Kabir, or the Great Mosque, in Gaza. Originally a church, which the Muslims enlarged and adapted to their needs, it was located in the east of the town

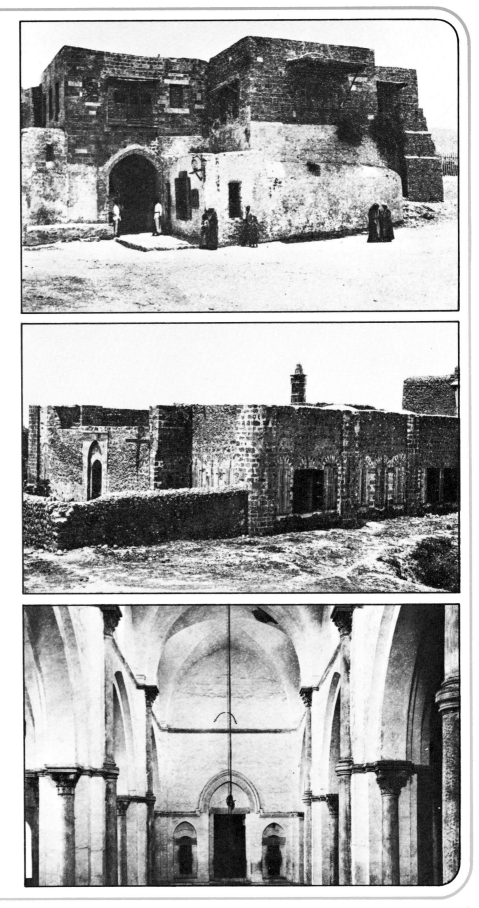

Nablus and environs

opposite
The ''Well of the Samaritan,'' of New
Testament fame, near Nablus

Nablus, the ancient Shechem, 1,870 feet (560 m.) above sea level,
lies in the valley between Mount Gerizim and Mount Ebal. Mount
Gerizim is almost 3,000 feet (900 m.) above sea level. The environs
are very fertile, and water abounds. The main center of the
Samaritan sect, Nablus had a market of some importance at the
time and traded with the area east of the Jordan River, especially
in wool and cotton. In the late nineteenth century it supported
twenty-two workshops that produced soap from olive oil. The
importance of Nablus for Ottoman rule is attested by the fact that it
already had a telegraph office on Abdul-Hamid's accession. At the
time, it was already a large urban center with about 12,000
inhabitants, mostly Muslims but also including about 600
Christians, 150 Samaritans, and 100 Jews. The population
continued to grow during Abdul-Hamid's reign. By comparison,
Samaria and Jenin were hardly more than poor villages at that
time.

right and overleaf
Two general views of Nablus, with
Mount Gerizim in the background

Samaria (Sebastia), though still containing several remnants of its ancient glory in Israelite and Roman days, was no more than a small, poor Arab village at the time

above
Beth-El, a town with biblical associations as "The House of God" and then "The House of Idols," was in Abdul-Hamid's days a poor Arab village with less than 500 inhabitants

right
An Arab peasant probably from the environs of Nablus

overleaf
Jenin, a small Arab town on the way from Samaria to Nazareth, had about 3,000 inhabitants, a spring which provided ample water, and good fruit

94

Galilee and the Haifa area

Galilee, although desolate in parts, was frequently visited by tourists in the late nineteenth century because of its religious significance for both Jews and Christians. The same was a reason for people of both religions to settle there. Tiberias was a case in point. After the 1839 earthquake, the town was largely restored with closely built houses on or near the shore of the Sea of Galilee, about 600-700 feet (200 m.) below sea level. The hot springs were heavily frequented at the time. At the start of Abdul-Hamid's reign, there were about 3,000 inhabitants in Tiberias, of whom half to two-thirds were Jews; and at its end there were almost 5,000, some 80 percent of whom were Jews. Near the end of the period, wider streets began to be built at the edge of Tiberias's old quarter on the seashore.

Capernaum (Hebrew, Kefar Nahum), on the northern shore of the Sea of Galilee, had been a thriving town in the days of Jesus, with whose activity it is associated in Christian tradition. In Abdul-Hamid's time it was in ruins. Kafr Kana, to which the New Testament ascribes Jesus' miracle of turning water into wine, is also in this area, about 3.8 miles (6 kms.) northeast of the Sea of Galilee.

Nazareth, a small town in Abdul-Hamid's days, was the capital of an administrative unit in the district of Acre. All of Nazareth's streets were narrow and steep; none was level or straight, but those in the center of town were paved with cobblestones. Like Jerusalem, Nazareth was a town in which various religious communities coexisted. On Abdul-Hamid's accession, it had a population of about 6,000, of whom about 2,000 were Muslims, 2,500 Greek Orthodox, 800 Roman Catholics, and the rest Maronites, Protestants, and members of other Christian sects. No Jews resided in Nazareth then, though some came to its markets. As a rule, the religious communities preferred to live in separate quarters. Almost all members of the Greek-Orthodox Church lived

Bedouin (probably from Galilee) drawing water. Here they were using the simplest, non-mechanical method — not even a wheel, just lowering buckets tied to ropes

overleaf
General view of Tiberias, rebuilt after the 1837 earthquake

right
The village of Kana in Galilee, believed
to be the site of the miracle of turning
water into wine

below
The Fountain of the Virgin in
Nazareth, an abundant spring near
which the Greek Orthodox built the
Church of the Annunciation. Such
springs served as meeting places for
the local women, who traded news
there

Capernaum (Hebrew, Kefar Nahum)
was in ruins in Abdul-Hamid's days.
The remains are seen here as they
were before archeologists reorganized
them

right
General view of Nazareth, the largest
urban center in central Galilee

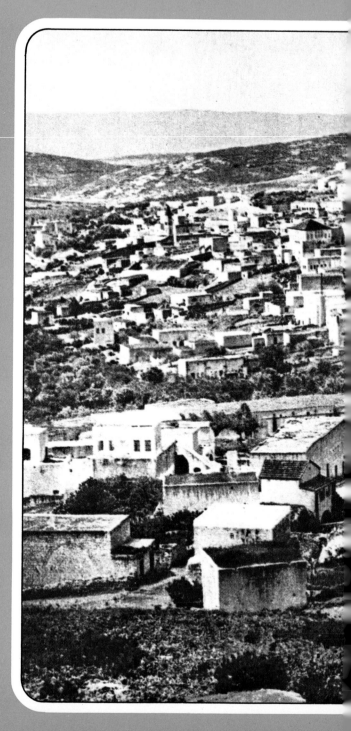

98

in the east end, the Roman Catholics with their religious associates — the Maronites and Greek Catholics — occupied the west, while a part of the center and the entire southern part of town were Muslim.

Acre, of Crusader fame, was an administrative center during the Ottoman period. Its heyday was in the late eighteenth century, thanks to its governor, Ahmad Jazzar Pasha, who ruled the area from 1775 to 1804 and maintained his residence in Acre. He rebuilt the walls and endowed Acre with public buildings, the most

overleaf
View of southern Galilee as seen from Mount Tabor (about 2,000 f., or 560 m., above sea level)

General view of Acre, with as-Suk al-Abyad ("The White Bazaar") in the center and the Great Mosque of Jazzar Pasha in the right background

General view of Haifa. Built mostly around the natural bay at the base of Mount Carmel, Haifa was then only beginning to grow into the international city it was to become in the twentieth century

renowned of which was the Great Mosque, named after him. In the nineteenth century, Acre was damaged in several military campaigns, but its status in the Ottoman administration and its preponderantly Muslim population still gave it a special standing. In Abdul-Hamid's era, however, it declined economically in favor of its rival, Haifa, which had a better protected port that was visited by steamers more frequently. On Abdul-Hamid's accession, Acre had approximately 8,000 inhabitants, of whom at least 5,600 were Muslims. Ten years later, Acre numbered about 9,000 souls, including some 140 Jews, and in 1894 close to 10,000, of whom 8,000 were apparently Muslims.

Haifa was destroyed and rebuilt several times; its present site dates from 1761. Its inhabitants lived off agriculture. From the mid-

nineteenth century, steamers increasingly began to patronize it, at the expense of Acre. The flow of money enabled people to build two-story houses, and in 1858 the first private homes beyond the wall surrounding the lower town were built on Mount Carmel. In the last third of the nineteenth century, there was a marked increase of the number of Christians in Haifa: German Templers, Catholic and Protestant missionaries, and businessmen. Haifa began to assume the look — a mixture of the local and international — that remained its hallmark during the late Ottoman period. In Abdul-Hamid's era it could boast of a dozen vice-consuls and consular agents of foreign states. Its population, which numbered about 6,000 in 1876, rose to nearly 18,000 at the end of Abdul-Hamid's reign in 1909. Its permanent residents, in addition to local Arabs and Jews, were a varied mix of Turks, Druze, Greeks, Italians, Armenians, and others. Its visitors comprised tourists, merchants, and sailors of many other nations. The Jews, whose number grew by immigration, played an increasing role in Haifa's public affairs and commercial life — side by side with a small but active European minority that added to Haifa's cosmopolitan character.

Mount Carmel. At the top left is Notre Dame du Mont-Carmel, built by the Carmelite Order at a point 560 feet (170 m.) above sea level. At the top right is the summer palace constructed near the lighthouse by 'Abdallah Pasha, governor of Acre, in 1821 and later taken over by the Carmelites and converted into a hostel (named Stella Maris). At the bottom right is the Cave of the Prophet Elijah, to whom the Jews attributed miraculous cures of mental illness and barrenness

Druze peasants at their meal in one of the villages on Mount Carmel. As was customary at the time, peasants—as well as Bedouin—ate with their fingers. One of the characteristic signs of Druze apparel was their headgear, turbans of snowy whiteness, compared to the white turban with a gold thread of the Muslims, the simple red fez of the Christians, and the broad-brimmed felt hats of the Jews.

Downtown Haifa near the seashore. This was the older part of Haifa in Abdul-Hamid's time, comprising the Harat al-Yahud or "Jewish Quarter"

Kaiser Wilhelm and his escort upon their arrival in Haifa on October 25, 1898. The site, on the outskirts of the city — popularly called "The Kaiser's Wharf" since then — was established specially so that the Kaiser and his escort could land near "The German Colony" of the Templers. The German press heralded the event by declaring that a German emperor had not landed in Palestine for 670 years

Holy Places

A section of the Via Dolorosa ("The Street of Pain") in Jerusalem, the route by which Jesus is believed to have borne his cross to Golgotha

Due to increasing and improved travel facilities in Abdul-Hamid's days, Palestine's holy places exerted an ever-growing attraction for pilgrims and tourists, while maintaining their appeal to the local population as well. Some of these places meant different things to different men. Thus St. Lazarus' Tomb in Bethany was a Christian holy site, but it was revered by the local Muslims too. In several other instances, places holy to various religions were in close proximity. For instance, the Great Mosque of Hebron is built above the Cave of the Patriarchs (Me'arat ha-Machpelah), considered by the Jews to be the burial place of their Patriarchs; and the Western ("Wailing") Wall of the Jews is part of the Temple Mount, in close proximity to al-Haram ash-Sharif of the Muslims. Various Christian denominations disputed their rights of possession and ritual at the Holy Sepulchre in Jerusalem — all of which only sharpened the curiosity and interest of the many visitors to the holy places in Palestine.

right and overleaf
Jews at prayer beside the Western ("Wailing") Wall in Jerusalem. This is a remnant of the supporting wall of the mount on which the holy Temple of the Jews was built

107

The Tomb of Rachel, near Bethlehem.
Revered by the Jews — and to a lesser
degree by Christians and Muslims — it
has been restored several times

Interior of The Great Mosque of Hebron, built over the Cave of the Patriarchs (Me'arat ha-Machpelah). Both Jews and Muslims revere the burial place of Abraham, Isaac, Jacob, and their wives. The mosque was jealously guarded, and in the nineteenth century the Muslims forbade members of other religions to go beyond its entrance. They believe that Isaac and Sarah are buried in the section of the mosque shown in this photograph

Interior of the Grotto and Manger, Bethlehem. In the large Church of the Nativity, built over the traditional birth place of Jesus, this is the most sacred spot and has been a focus of Christian pilgrimage to Palestine for many generations

left
Tomb of St. Lazarus, Bethany. According to Christian tradition, this was the site of the Tomb of St. Lazarus, whom Jesus brought back to life. Steps descend to the burial chamber

opposite
Ecce Homo Arch in the Via Dolorosa, where Pilate is said to have pointed at Jesus and said, ''This is the man!'' Consequently, the arch was sometimes known as the Arch of Pilate

The Garden of Gethsemane (in Aramaic, "oil-press") in Jerusalem. In Abdul-Hamid's days, the garden still boasted several ancient olive trees, alleged to have witnessed Jesus' arrest. Today it is a part of the Basilica of Gethsemane, on the lower slope of the Mount of Olives

The Tomb of the Virgin, Jerusalem. This is the principal façade of the chapel (facing south) on the road near the Valley of Kidron. The chapel was built by Milicent, daughter of King Baldwin II and wife of Fulk of Anjou, of Crusader fame

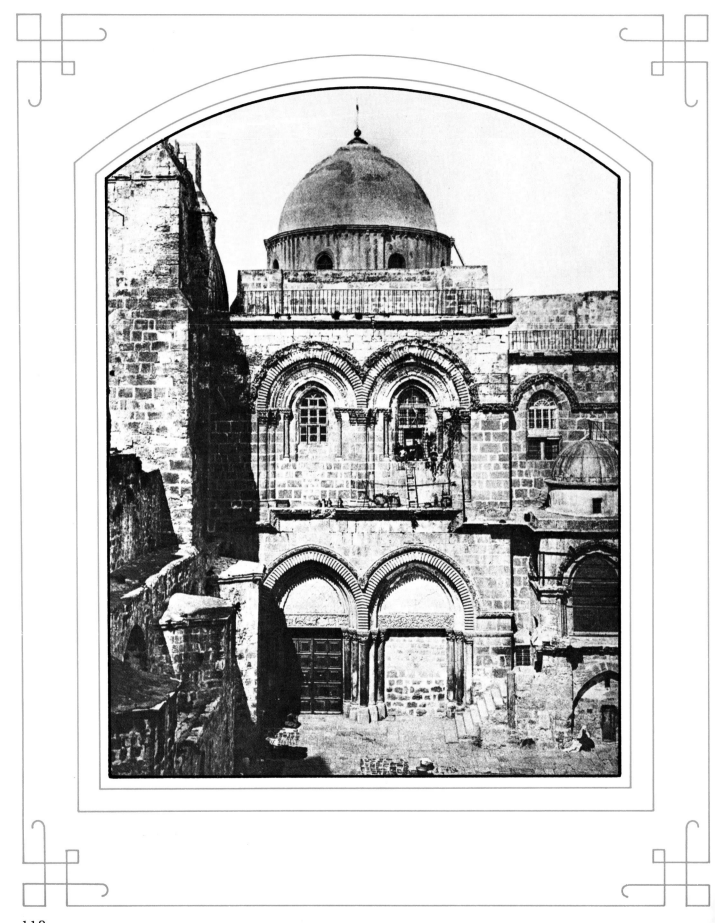

right
The Greek-Orthodox feet-washing
ceremony in front of the Church of the
Holy Sepulchre on Holy Thursday

opposite
Façade of the Church of the Holy
Sepulchre, Jerusalem, a complex of
several buildings situated on a site
identified in Christian tradition as
Golgotha. The photograph shows the
main entrance, facing south. The bas-
relief over the left portal represented
scenes from the New Testament,
while the right portal was walled up,
and in front a stairway ascended to
the Chapel of Calvary

Exterior of al-Aksa Mosque ("The Farthest Mosque"), Jerusalem. This complex of buildings in al-Haram ash-Sharif ("The Noble Sanctuary") on Mount Moriah was built in the early eighth century and was subsequently embellished by several Muslim rulers

Minbar as-Sayf ("The Summer Pulpit") between al-Aksa and the Dome of the Rock, so called because it was used for preaching — chiefly on Friday noon — during the summer. Its other name was The Pulpit of Burhan ad-Din, after the Arab judge of that name who used to preach from it in the fourteenth century C.E.

opposite
Interior of the Dome of the Rock. Many of the decorations are from the era of Saladin, who ordered the mosque restored as soon as he had reconquered Jerusalem from the Crusaders in 1187. Muslim tradition has it that the Prophet Muhammad prayed here and was then transported from the holy rock to heaven on his steed

A *çeşme,* or basin, south of the Dome of the Rock. Donated as a gift by Abdul-Hamid II, it served for the washing of hands and feet before entering the mosque to pray

left, below
Exterior of the Dome of the Rock (The Mosque of Omar) in al-Haram ash-Sharif. Built on the summit of Mount Moriah in 691 C.E., it is a large and handsome octagon, covered with fine porcelain tiles as far as the pedestal and with marble lower down

People and Professions

opposite
A Jerusalem Jew dressed in
traditional garb

The human landscape of Abdul-Hamid's Palestine complemented
the natural one in its color, variety, and contrast. The mixture of
religious and ethnic groups, peasants and Bedouin, missionaries
and representatives of foreign governments must have added
greatly to the fascination that the country exercised over the
visitor. While the local population engaged in all types of
occupations, those encountered most frequently dealt with such
necessities of life as purveying food and drink, supplying building
materials, repairing clothing and shoes, and providing means of
transport. It was these occupations that maintained the country's
specific local flavor because of their stubbornly preserved ties to the
past.

right
Arab women from Bethlehem dressed
in their finery

opposite
A group of religious Jews in Jerusalem

right
A girl from Bethlehem in her fine
clothes and jewelry — the latter made
of Ottoman coins strung together. In
Palestine at that time, money was not
put in the bank. Arabs either buried it
or turned it into jewelry to be worn by
their women, who thus became
''ambulatory banks''

127

The Arab sheikh of a Palestinian village. Sheikh literally means "an old man" in Arabic. Until Abdul-Hamid's reign, village sheikhs had considerable authority; but under his rule, the Ottoman government acted to curtail the direct power of these elders

Peasant women from Jerusalem

Girls from peasant families living in the vicinity of Jerusalem selling their produce

A group of peasants from the village of Silwan, near Jerusalem, dressed in the traditional white robe, or *kumbaz*, and black cloak, or *'abaya*

Bedouin from the area east of the
Jordan River

Bedouin women and children before
their tents. The clothes worn by the
children were generally very simple,
except for an occasional ornate cap

right
Bedouin from the environs of the
village of Silwan

opposite
Bedouin women with their children.
Note the tatoo on the face of the
woman on the right and — a sign of
changing times — the shoes worn by
the other

opposite
A Jerusalem water carrier. Such a waterskin usually contained between 6.6 gallons (25 liters) and 10.6 gallons (40 liters). Pure water was usually in great demand, since it was frequently unavailable in Jerusalem (and elsewhere in Palestine); unless drawn from a spring, it was often contaminated

Bread vendors in Jerusalem. Bread was the staple food of the Arab population in Palestine, especially of the peasants

A cobbler and his customers in Jerusalem. Shoes were increasingly worn by the local people in Abdul-Hamid's time. While town cobblers produced the better quality shoes, those in the larger villages catered to the well to do with the rougher, heavier kinds, the uppers made of sheepskin and the soles of camel hides. Many cobblers made their living by moving from village to village repairing shoes

Stonemasons from Jerusalem (or Bethlehem) and porters who carried the finished product. Quarrying was largely carried out in the hill country, often in the neighborhood of towns. In addition to gunpowder, large hammers were used, aided when necessary by iron wedges

Peasants of Silwan, a village near Jerusalem, selling homemade sour milk, another popular staple

A peasant in Galilee kneading the dough for bread. This was usually done in the early morning, so that the menfolk could take freshly baked bread with them

Women peasants grinding wheat in Jerusalem. In contrast to the villagers, who generally ground the wheat grains by hand and produced a coarser bread, townspeople — particularly the well to do — used two round millstones to grind more finely and bake a more delicate bread.

There were no roads for carts or carriages in most of the areas of Palestine, so that all the heavy transport was effected by means of camels. They carried nearly all the stones quarried for building in Jerusalem, for example, or the grain brought from the rich cornfields near the Jordan River to the coastal towns

The boatmen in the Jaffa harbor made
their living by transporting people
from the ships — which dropped
anchor in the port, away from the
rocks — to the shore and vice versa

Index